About the Author

George Hobson is a priest in the Episcopal/Anglican Church. He has lived in France for over half his life, working with both French and English-speaking churches. He studied theology at Oxford in the 1980s and earned his doctorate in 1989. From 1995 to 2000 he held the post of Canon Pastor at the American Cathedral in Paris. With his wife Victoria he has travelled extensively in developing countries, notably Rwanda, Haiti, Pakistan, and Armenia, teaching courses in theological colleges. His first book of poetry, illustrated with his own art photographs, was published in England in 2005. Since then, with Wipf and Stock, he has published two books of theological/social analysis and four volumes of poetry: *The Parthenon, May Day Morning in Yerevan, Heights and Depths*, and *A Far Country Here*. His poem Sun Patch won Second Prize in the International Bridport Poetry Competition in 1995.

Love Poems for My Wife, Victoria

George Hobson

Love Poems for My Wife, Victoria

RESOURCE *Publications* • Eugene, Oregon

Resource Publications
A division of Wipf and Stock Publishers
199 W 8th Ave, Suite 3
Eugene, OR 97401

Love Poems for My Wife, Victoria
By Hobson, George
Copyright © 2019 by Hobson, George All rights reserved.
Softcover ISBN-13: 979-8-3852-1435-8
Hardcover ISBN-13: 979-8-3852-1436-5
eBook ISBN-13: 979-8-3852-1437-2
Publication date 1/23/2024
Previously published by Olympia Publishers, 2019

This edition is a scanned facsimile of the original edition published in 2019.

Dedication

For my wonderful Victoria, God's precious gift to me in this life, whom I cherish and shall cherish forever in the fullness of the life to come.

Acknowledgements

I owe an enormous debt to John Paris, dear friend of fifty years and brother in Christ. Long before Victoria and I were married, it was he who first spoke the Christian gospel to her and later to me with conviction and authority and his own changed life as a testimony to its truth power. In the first year of our marriage, John prayed with and for Victoria and me frequently and helped to train us for the pastoral lay ministry we would later exercise together in America and France. His singular intelligence and spiritual sensitivity have been a blessing to us over the years whenever we have been able to be together. And in the last two years, through countless exchanges, he has sustained me in my passionate cry to God to heal my beloved wife and restore her to me. Through assiduous prayer and wise counsel, John has contributed significantly to the deepening love between Victoria and me during this long trial. Thank you, dear brother, for making us beneficiaries in so many ways, for over half a century, of your own steadfast love of our Lord Jesus Christ.

Forward

In these tender poems, ranging over decades, George shares many life experiences as the devoted husband of a wonderful woman. The poems are a buoyant mixture of lyrical tones and forms, including narratives, dialogues and traditional sonnets. They trace the radical impact of marriage on the two young lovers; the considerable accommodations needed to build a solid foundation for their lives together; the pain of occasional geographical separation; the increasing maturity of both spouses and their deepening appreciation of each other as they live out complex lives, and the massive challenge of Victoria's memory problem as it emerges in the fifth decade of their union. I could almost *feel* the growth of their love as I read through these poignant lyrics.

I personally was privileged to be blessed by their company on one of our pilgrimages in the historically Armenian Christian land of Nagorno Karabakh, and, on another occasion, by the opportunity, at their invitation, to speak in the American Cathedral in Paris at a conference Victoria organized in 2001 to celebrate the 1700th Anniversary of the birth of Armenia as a Christian nation. So I have had a number of chances to witness their deep devotion to each other. George himself captures succinctly the springs of this devotion in *The Psaltery* (IX), the second long poem in his remarkable recent collection entitled *Faces of Memory*, a volume that, in epic form, enshrines the whole spectrum of human emotions, from the terror of man's inhumanity to man—such as the horrific description of suffering inflicted in the Rwandan Genocide—to the tenderness of human love and the infinite hope we can experience in the love of God. He writes: "They are two, but knotted./ It is their bondedness that counts,/ That makes them what they are:/ Two in one, one in two:/ *Foldedness, unfolding, infolding, dropping.*"

Victoria is now suffering to some degree from memory loss, and George wishes to dedicate this book of love poems to her, trusting that Love will continue to bring its healing power. It is well known that such love transcends problems of communication and normal comprehension, as he and Victoria are experiencing every day. Therefore, I trust, with them, that these poems—this gift of love—will bring deep comfort and ongoing restoration to the Victoria whom George cherishes, enshrining the timeless truth "Ubi Caritas? Where Love is, God is."

I pray that both Victoria and George will be abundantly blessed by this love.

Caroline Cox
(Baroness Cox, of Queensbury in Greater London)

You Shall Cherish Her

Love settled on the smile across the room
And said: This is she. You shall cherish her
All your years: her radiance today,
Her beauty in the middle passage, her loveliness
In age. She is yours to keep and hold.
Her smile is like a leaf in morning sun,
Her laughter like water burbling over stones;
Her heart is glass, transparent; her will
A compass, fixed to do the bidding of her Lord.
Cherish her, she is woman, she is yours.
You must endure the strain of time. Each trial
Will be occasion for your love to grow.
This woman is my gift, says God. Take her as wife.
In her beauty lies the mirror of eternal life.

Three Photographs

I

How is it I scarcely saw you
All those years ago?
What cataracts filmed my eyes
As I gazed where you stood ankle-deep
In the shallows of the Great Lake,
Your right leg cocked,
The left, like a column, bearing you,
Hip curved out sensually,
Your long arms holding up the hem of your blue print dress
From the shadowed water by the shore,
While your hair fell in waves down the side of your face
To your shoulder?
How could my whole soul and body fail to exult
At the kindness in your hazelnut eyes
And the smile playing on your face,
Warm, mischievous and gentle,
Like the cusp of the new moon
South of the Equator?
"I am woman," said the smile.
"I am your helpmate, your lover and friend.
You are man,

My man,
My husband.
I love you."
Yes.
The truth of your words was deep in my heart,
Like a bulb buried in a garden;
But the words themselves—
Alas!—
They flew through my mind
Like birds through the space outside my window:
I saw shapes, heard flapping wings—
Quick my heart!—
But then silence.
I do not say they did not leave a trace;
I do not say there was no link
Between bulb and birds,
Between truth and the words
Your warm smile spoke.
But the knowledge that I am loved of God,
And the good love of self rooted in that knowledge,
Was not yet mine,
Or was glimpsed only at a distance, briefly,
As lightning, splitting dark,
Illuminates the land,
And one sees it for an instant as it is,
Mass and form revealed in beauty,
Before night comes down again,
Before blindness falls again,
And one can no longer imagine the world under light.
You knew—

You were the first to know—
Without that good self-love
I could not love you as I wished
Or take your love simply.
As I wished!
As my body—my whole being—longed to do!
As my heart—where my real love lay buried—longed to do!
To see you truly—and to give you love—
Oh, so simple, simple, simple!
But how could I see you all those years ago,
Crippled as I was?

II

And here you are again, after another eight years,
On a wide beach in Brittany pleated by wavelets,
Your shape moulded by that bathing suit we liked
(Motifs of red and green on a white ground—remember?),
Head tipped slightly
(As at the Great Lake),
Fair hair falling in the same waves to the same shoulder
(Against a distant backdrop of white cliffs and ocean)
And the same smile that claimed me, saying:
"I am woman,
You are mine.
You are learning to love and be loved,
I will not let you go."
Oh, wife of my youth!
How vain from our years' hilltop
To regret my failure to know you
With my whole soul and body
When we were still young.

What counts is our faithfulness
And the slow growth of love:
So is true passion nourished.

The carousel turns;

Leaves bud, open, drop,
Bud anew, open, drop;
And our brows show small lines,
Our hair greys,
Our backs ache in the morning,
And the stairs we climb each day grow steeper,
And our breath each day grows shorter.
Ah, my dearest—!
Woman!
Wife!
How I would our youth were ours again—
Ours in our age!
For our passion is richer now than then,
Our intimacy truer.
Our Lord has kept us from falling,
Even when it seemed we were straying
Near the cliff-edge.
And we have learned—
We two have learned—
Something of faithfulness
And something of death
To the bad self-love
That insists it is right,
That demands approbation.
Though the seasons have turned,
Though the leaves have flourished and fallen,
The rings of our tree have increased,
The trunk has thickened and strengthened,
Our roots have gone deeper
Into love's loamy soil.

III

Shall I not now give thanks to God and you—
My love, my woman!—
Whom I see laughing here in a Middle-Eastern land
Where the Saviour walked once,
Your head thrown back,
Hair straggly in the wind,
Your left arm raised in abandon,
Carefree, wild,
The kind of gesture I love,
The kind of gesture I love you for—
Shall I not give thanks?
Behind you an ancient fortress
With crenellations and slits to shoot from,
Picture of my old soul
As it was when we met,
Before you and my Lord
Assaulted and captured my stronghold,
Set up house within its walls,
Refurbished it slowly,
And made it an inn.
Oh, yes, I give *thanks*!
I shall sing thanks to heaven,
And to you speak it sweetly—
Any veil left between us

Will be rent by the echo.
Where I sit now, Love, in Rwanda,
Banana leaves tremble near my window
And towering eucalyptus play their scales on the sky.
I think of you in Paris,
Full of life,
Teaching, praying, phoning, putting order.
And behind you in my mind's eye rise up,
Like these great green banana fronds around me,
Crowds of figures from our past,
Standing here, there, everywhere,
Rustling in the wind of memory.
They come forward to greet us,
Waving at us gladly,
Waving at the two of us together,
George and Victoria,
As we walk hand in hand through the dense green forest,
Rejoicing.

Victoria

Do I call you most tellingly my "love" or "wife"?
You lured me, Love, as land the venturer
On open seas. I spied afar fresh fruit, a life
Delightful, incandescent, you the bearer
Of good grain, blond wheat sheaf in my shadowy
Hold. We spoke the solemn words: my wife
You were declared to be, dear wearer
Of my ring. Patiently you steadied me,
You broke the two-edged blade, you made
Of me a husband. Awkward seaman, I wasn't handy
In a home; accustomed to the wild sea's swell
And toss, the rodeo of waves, I swayed
And rocked for years, leading you on a wet hell
Of a journey, on and off. Boldly you stayed
Me, brooked the roaring storm; you stood
Against the winds that howled through the pell-mell
Chaos of my rigging: you, sheaf in my wildwood
Scattering seed, making slowly a farmer
Of me, a courteous landsman, breaking the moods
That overcast my skies like grey fog's hood.
Doggedly, bravely, you nudged me into warmer
Climes, towed me toward serener latitudes.
Of God's compelling love you became the informer
Of my soul: in the sea-wet spaces of my solitude

You anchored, and abode; in my cracked vessel you became
Yourself, sure conduit of God's power, by which He drowned
    Slowly, over years, the thick-encrusted scum
    Of a life-time's ocean errancy. My ship
You brought some order to, and made your home: sound
Beams you saw me lay among the rotting timbers, wholesome
    Fare you set upon my board—and we weathered the trip
    Of years, of long leagues, by night and day, to land.
So were you my wife: in relationship
To me of stay and succour, true and steadfast friend,
    Of the false in my old heart the stalwart foe:
    Thus was your love tested, and mine made real.
I said "my love" at first, but facilely; now, tanned
    By time's heat and bright day's glare, aglow
    With ruddy colour won in struggle to be loyal,
I honour you and call you knowingly "my wife". But oh,
    The love locked up in that warm word
    Upon my lips! For if I've learned earth's soil
    To till with patient hand; if fruit and honey
    Now are mine and the harsh lurch seaward
Of my life is turned, it's you I owe it to, whose sunny
    Eyes held me in day and lanced the absurd
    Tumescent darkness of my soul. With me you,
    Blond wheat sheaf, in my ship's hold steamy
With the wet of sea and tears, abode; our young dream
    Of laughing love you put aside a time—in lieu
    You shouldered *me*! Christ's image, you, dear, gleam
    With his bright light; in his fair retinue,
    By grace of God, you've held, do hold me fast—
You, my love, have brought me into your glad home at last.

Our Love

I have not always loved you true,
But I have always loved you. Unpleasant
Odours in my cabin needed flushing out, blue
Walls needed livening up, the elephant
In the dining room needed proper instruction.
You had to open windows to let the air in.
You know, dear one, I didn't find contrition
Easy, before God or you; nor was sin
Only mine, as you agree; the righteous "I"
That judged the likes of me had staked a claim
In you as well. But you were quick to die
To pride, as Light revealed it. The great Name
Of Jesus is your joy; your heart's desire,
To do his will, which is love. His life in you
Has filled your own life with love, set fire
To your days. You've been my crackling hearth through
The middle years, warming me, softening me;
And as we age, your presence, like perfume,
Makes my life sweet, your goodness sets me free—
My own love, like a flower, is made by yours to bloom.

Love

I sit in the room with our handicapped kitten,
A fur-ball the colour of cinnamon toast,
Spooning him food on my lap as he sinks towards death.
When I hold him, or my wife does, he's happy;
Our hands on his haunches or head calm his fear,
Stop his shaking; the sense of his oddness
Is lifted; he rests in our presence, purring,
Secure in our love.

O kitty, be our example!
May we linger like you in the love
Of our Father who made us,
A love greater than death, which passes,
A love greater than pain, which dies.

Love speaks "*You!*" to each creature:
Precious, invaluable being,
Beyond general classes and measures,
Kitty, colour of tweed, twitching in sleep,
Hydrocephalic, crippled from birth—
Sweet beast, you are loved!
And I and you too, my companion, my wife,
Partner on our way through this canyon

Of barbarous shadows—
We are cherished by God!
Oh, may we cleave to his grace!
May our hearts know his peace!

This valley of horror,
This ruined heath,
This bog, this bloody fen
Where murderers stalk,
This haunt of fetid souls,
This lot, this mall,
This concrete block
Where dealers skulk
And addicts slouch:
Even in this desolate
Sin-wrecked world,
In this den, this morgue,
God reaches out to
His fallen creatures
And offers us life:
He dwells here in love.

Love strips habit's film from our eyes,
Brings each being's beauty to light:
This creature, that,
This particular cat,
This tomato, that walnut, this dog.
And we in God's image,
Who indwell his order,
Can name them

And know them
And enfold them in love.
Oh, glory!
For we have been named and been known
First of all.

Love came to my soul and said, "Come",
And to yours, dear, and said, "Come":
And to you whom I've failed to love fully,
And to me whom you've tried to love fully,
Shall be given the fullness of union
That rose in our hearts like a vision
In a party in Upper Manhattan long ago,
When my eyes caught a glimpse of you standing,
Your face like a pearl in the lamplight,
Across a room full of voices and laughter,
And I eased in a dream to your side
Like one borne on an incoming tide
To a comforting shore.
In the world to come, sweet lady, wife
(And even now, partly, by grace's might),
The buds of the love glimpsed briefly then—
To be battered soon by tempestuous winds
And seared by the harsh frost of anger
From earlier days, unpurged, vented on you—
Will flower in joy;
And laughter will rise again
As it did in those first blushing weeks
When we were still young
(Brief flame on the water!),

When your name in my ears
(And mine in yours!)
Was like the thrush's golden song at dawn
Publishing a plenitude of love
In echo of the first glad Day
And of the Last,
When all the angels
And the whole creation
Sang to God
And will sing
And will go on singing
Forever.

Learn to Love Her Better, Friend

Learn to love her better, friend: the lower
chamber of the hourglass is filling fast, sand-
grains are pouring through the channel, hour
by hour. No *tour de force,* nor sleight of hand,
nor even prayer, will stay their course.
Learn quickly, friend, to love her better.
Those strong arms, carrying, cleaning, scrubbing,
won't return forever to their daily chores.
One day,
the wrongs she seeks to right, the texts to edit, the wood
wanting polishing, the pot-shards glueing, the weeds
to pull up, the roses to prune: all those good
tasks won't get done any more, nor countless seeds
be sown any more, for this great carer's strength
will have failed.
So look to it, friend, don't wait,
learn to love her better while you've time. The length
of days is shortening for you both, the hour is late.
Yank your weeds of dullness, uproot regrets,
haul out those old rocks of grievance. No fate
forces them upon you, no mean God up there lets
you dangle on a rope. The game is yours to play.
Learn to love her better, friend, while you may.

The Painting

You wake. Beyond the window a picture:
Brown green yellow slathers of oil paint
Devising tilted fields. Beneath bulbous
Green flames flaring like the mantles
Of kerosene lamps lie pools of shadow,
Blue discs among the rectilinear
Strokes of unctuous paint. So behold:
Colours shape, planes define: there is square,
There is round: there are angles, curves,
Solids, voids, points—and it is good.

You look. A patch of pale green is barley,
It ruffles under wind like the corduroy
Surface of a broad bay when breezes freshen.
A swatch of yellow is wheat. A tile the shade
Of nutmeg is a ploughed field, another—
Unploughed—is cinnamon. On all the textures
The sheen is the sun's gift, diffused like love.
So there is rough in the painting, and smooth;
There is light, there is dark—and it is good.

You sleep, you wake. You rub your eyes. A stroke
Of beige, curving, makes a figure: *woman*.

Oh, she is bell bowl bulb
Blown glass
Birdsong
Marble ivory alabaster jade
She is gourd
Jug
A birch-tree trunk
Acacia
She is lily
She is fruit
A pear on a brown ground—
Flesh:
She is *woman*.

You dream. She and you are in the picture
Running, and yet you do not move, you are
Motionless. Together you gather up space,
Focus it, open it outward, inward.
You are two making one, one in two,
Strokes of paint on a white ground, dreamed.

Time halts here. Together you and she wade
In the yellow, the wheat; you skip across
The tilted hill, breach the blue space called sky,
Dance round and round among the green flames.
You throw back your heads, you exult .And yet
You are at rest the while, motionless;
And the wind in the barley is your laughter.

You wake. The curved stroke of beige on the canvas
Beyond the window where you sit, shimmers.
Woman. She is a gift to you. Love her.
She is beauty. She is like and unlike you.

You smile—and you see that it is *very good.*

Rest

We who have given so much to others
In God-sent labour (how should I, poor
Egoist, otherwise give love?)
Receive now, each for the other, time
And a disposition to enjoy.

Days like leaves in the still air turn,
Streams in the mountains tumble, but we
Do not hear them, not now, for we have become
Like them, not changing, though we have been changed.
Nature knows not time.

Love poured so long by you, my love,
Upon my heart's cracked rock, finds—O wonder!—
Finally the granite grooved and smooth,
Chaos of mountain birth breached:
Old rock made new.

Here, yes, is change, here has been change,
Not the streams, not your love, dear—
My heart's stone, rather: so God
By you on me has worked, by grace
Fitting broken me to love.

Pictures come to us of those by our poor labours
Aided, gnawed bones of a carnivorous age.
We hear again the bursts and tearful mutterings
Of the maimed ones with injured hearts, whom love
Releases into speech and hope.

Oh, the tales told, the wail and weep of it!
Yet here have we gone too, you and I:
"Father, forgive me; Father, I forgive…"
We too have spoken, confessed, decided;
Have humbled ourselves and prayed. So now

High birds soar on the Breughelian canvas
Above the restive clamour, the melancholy fêtes:
Wide-winged, they staple the sky to the huts
And hills below and lift to heaven's peace
The pandemonium of our time.

Days like leaves in the still air turning:
Inside their cicada-throb we lie
Quiet, and receive. We rest. Love
Turns helpless time into eternity, redeems it:
Thus are all things ours, and we Christ's.

Castelnau

I feel your hand on my shoulder as we stand by the fence
Listening to the cows munching grass.
The field slopes up behind them into woods
That climb to the top of the hill and the castle.
A huge bulk,
The castle is way out of proportion with the scene below:
The cows, the grass, the wire fence,
Your hand on my shoulder as we listen to the cows munching.

It was a dream, wasn't it, Love, those years
Lived in the shadow of Castelnau,
A pile of red rock poised above Prudhommat
Near the bastide of Bretenoux, where the Cère,
Draining the high hills of the Cantal,
Joins the Dordogne to flow westward
By the limestone cliffs of the Perigord,
Through the wine-lands beyond Bergerac,
To the estuary of the Gironde and the ocean?

Wasn't it a dream?

We strung our laundry by a poplar grove in sight of the castle,
Where the first baron of Castelnau

Built a crenelated dungeon tower in the Thirteenth Century,
While Simon de Montfort slaughtered Albigensians
In the region to the south called the Pays d'Oc,
The land where the troubadours sang of courtly love
In the High Middle Ages.

We cannot sing today of courtly love.
It is hard today to sing of any kind of love at all
Except it be Christ's love,
The love of self-sacrifice
In the midst of bullets and fire.

Cannonballs brought an end to the age of fortified castles;
By the Seventeenth Century Castelnau was a relic.
Today bombs would make short work of the castle,
A drone would sniff out the baron and destroy him.
In feudal times the barons of Castelnau
Fought the nearby counts of Turenne
For supremacy in the region.
Today the castle is owned by the State
And open to tourists.
On guided visits, if you listen carefully,
You can hear the gruff talk of the lords in the Hall,
Or their footsteps on the stone staircase in the tower,
Perhaps the whisper of their ladies in the private quarters,
Or even the prayers of the knights in the chapel
As they cross themselves and prepare for battle.
But you must listen carefully,
The voices in the walls are faint,
The thunder of fighter planes ripping up the sky
On manoeuvres out of Toulouse
Easily drowns them out.

For four years the Dordogne flowed by us
Just beyond the copse of poplars.
We fetched milk from a local farmer
And bought supplies in Bretenoux,
The new town founded in 1277
By Guérin de Castelnau.
Two litters of kittens arrived and departed,
People of all sorts came and went.
By winter nights we huddled near the hearth
And spoke of Christ's mercy and power.
We made love in a wide bed
And listened to the wind in the poplars.
Sometimes at night we saw lights high up in the castle.
Perhaps the barons were feasting in the Hall.
We stared up at the lighted windows from the plain.
It was the Fourteenth Century.
We were vassals, tending the land for our feudal lord,
The Baron of Castelnau.
How grand were the battlements!
How imposing the tower!
And see the pennant of Castelnau
Flapping in the wind on the ramparts!
As we stared, a satellite orbiting earth far above the castle
Caught our eye as it blinked in its course.
Then the lights in the castle went out.

For four years we lived in the shadow of Castelnau
Near Prudhommat on the River Cère.
It was a dream, my Love, wasn't it?

Summer's End

All day long clouds roll
Through the blue air, rank on rank,
Marking summer's end, the changing of the guard,
Autumn's coming and the year's solemn fall.

All day long I watch them sail,
Baroque shapes in the enormous sky:
Fleece-figures, magnified by air,
Mirroring tree-clumps on Burgundian hills.

Our August, Love, is sped away,
The plums of yet another year are picked;
Yesterday's storms have washed the sky—
Today the air is sharp: September's here!

The summer clouds retreat and stain the land
(Blood runs down the stubbled fields!);
Crows are cawing, and corn-stalks, bent
Like donkeys' ears, are trembling in the wind.

Oh, my Love, the years are passing by!
We run to meet them, dancing
To their patterns, spinning down their days:
They play our inborn music on the sky.

But then, like songs, they're gone! Oh, hearts grow sad,
Seasons turning end on end…
We long for God, Framer of the rolling years,
Of us as well: we know that our Redeemer lives.

In Him, my Love, we know we'll never die:
No clouds will mark the waning
Of our days, nor wind strip bare our trunks
Or pinch our hearts: our Lord will guard our lives.

Our Lord, my Love, will keep these earthly years,
Our treasured memories He'll hold
Within His hand; no worms will eat
These dear beginnings here below of Life in Him.

All beauty seen, all love received
And shown, all truth upheld,
All joys we've shared together, dearest Love,
Will stand forever in our Saviour's Kingdom come.

Two in One

I rehearsed my life with you, near thirty years,
And saw it like a bamboo shaft, in segments,
Each from each angling off, as it had been ears
Of corn joined together, zig-zagging, fragments
Making up a kind of cord across
My memory, yet each as well a whole,
So that when some were lean, what seemed a loss
To our love, like the English stretch, had a role
To play, vital to our union, missing which
Our motley lives would lack the shape they have,
Peculiar as it is, an entwining rich
And poor at once, both frayed and tensile, a love
Like any worth the name, where two have wound
Themselves in one, by trust and pity bound.

Thoughts in Absence

Seven weeks have passed since I've been gone
From you, and you from me; yet all the while,
Though I be here, you there, my thoughts have run
To join you and take comfort in your smile.
On stormy nights, when thunder shakes my heart,
I pitch my tent near you and brave the blast;
When morning comes, and duties make me part
From you a time, your love holds me fast.
So night and day I company with you,
Though mountain, sea, and desert stand between;
For thoughts borne by love, love by thoughts, undo
The many miles, from tyrant space us wean.
But when I soon shall see you once again,
Then thoughts like these I'll need no longer pen.

For My True Love

Love, you're all about me. Everywhere
I see your hand and eye. Your strong heart beats
In every corner of the empty house; your care
Covers every object my dull gaze meets.
The rug, the fire-tools, the re-upholstered chairs,
The table freshly waxed, the bedspread stitched,
The hanging baskets, jam-jars, bowls—each wears
Your stamp, as if your heart's workshop, love-rich,
Had made them all from scratch. Where your hand
Falls, comes colour! Cook, knit, wash, mend—life springs
Up! Things dance. Words play. Your exciting land
Laughs. Dig, plant—dahlias burst out! What you touch sings.
Oh, Love, when you're away, as now, the house is sad;
But your smile, ringing me round, makes my heart glad.

You Absent

When you are absent, the joys we've known together
Come on-stage and begin to dance.
With the lightness of feathers
They leap from the wings and prance
Across the boards, lithesome memories
That slumber, when you're here, behind
The ordinary sets and scenery
Of our common lives, entwined.
If I imagine that you don't come back;
If I imagine that you die and go to be
With God, the joys go dark, mourn, crack
In two, the one part fixed in the lee
Of time's charge, the other turned
Into a knife, stabbing my heart.
The joys undone, broken, the stage seems a burnt
Plain, vast and bleak, where phantoms dart
Among the ashes and no life stirs.
Those joys were *shared*. You gone from me,
They rise before my eyes like empty towers
Whose lights have all gone black. Ah, memory:
My Love with me, you're a deep well
Filled with water; she gone, you're hell.

You Gone, Beauty Leaves me Cold

You gone, beauty leaves me cold.
Even truth's unhinged and seems a cold thing.
It's love makes life,
all else is seasoning.
Your presence absent, reality deflates:
hills contract to silhouettes;
trees, once statements of order,
are tangles of disheveled hair;
roads lead nowhere,
birds sing off-key,
flowers are black,
roses smell sour:
the heart becomes a winter landscape,
sans colour, *sans* form, *sans* everything.

Yes, it's like old age.
Yet not so, for old age graced by the beloved's presence,
though overcast by coming separation,
still displays the jewel of love
that makes all things created shine.
The one I love is there to gaze upon,
to sit beside and touch;
a hand is there to hold,

an arm to grasp,
cheek to kiss;
together we remember brighter times and smile.
You gone, there's nothing.
The fire dead, neither heat nor light remains:
ash is all.
Beauty unshared holds no intrinsic thrill.
The world is love's work, God's work:
each thread is for another,
stitched for another.
Reality is bondedness.
You gone, creation seizes up.
The heart becomes a frozen pond
where the leaves and roots and limbs of trees
that filled our years
are gripped in ice,
inert,
memories turned to mere matter
that must soon decay.

Yet in Christ we have hope.
My loss now,
or yours,
or our last loss someday,
is not the final word.
God will see his will performed on earth
as it is in heaven.
When Christ returns,
we'll see him as he is
and each other as we truly are,

as we were made to be.
What will be gone *then*,
what will be no more *then*,
is absence—
for you, my Lord, who are love,
will be *present*;
you will have trampled down dark death forever,
loss will be gone,
you'll be our all in all,
our Lord,
our love,
forever and forever.

Communion

In this silence we commune. Now we say more
Than words speak. Yet we need words to draw out
All the love our hearts contain. On time's shore
We stand, attending to life, going about
The business of living in the modern age.
It is difficult today to inhabit silence.
Time's a speeding rocket, space a cage
Full of febrile clamour. Night, immense,
Once the sheath of silence, lies ruined now
With noise and neon. Populations rave.
But you and I are called to peace. We vow
Love in the silence of our hearts. From a cave
Of quiet, its rock walls carved with words
From the countless songs we've sung, we take flight
Beyond words, beyond our dear songs, like birds
Lifting from earth into open sky, scaling light.

The Scent of Night

Magnolias cup the air in soft hands,
Filling the summer night with warm perfume,
While lights across the wide bay figure
Fiery stars embroidering heaven's cloak.

Dreams are floating in the pungent air
Like buds of the redolent magnolia,
Intimating unbruised worlds concealed
Beyond earth's edge and ocean's watery rim.

White sails resembling butterflies
Were flitting all day long on the blue sea,
Like velvet petals on the slate terrace
Pushed to and fro by playful puffs of wind.

Pines like Indian dancers, limbs looped
In buckles and hoops, now stand stilly dark
Against the still more dark black night,
While stars like live sparks lodge in their tops.

All day long the yellow blooms of broom
Mirrored the buoys of the sailboats
Moored in the bay, and now, together,
All have melted into shapeless air.

Wavelets lisp across the pebbly shore
While limes whisper cautiously, or pray
To their Creator with the generous love
    Of trees, offering leafy incense.

Sleep is night's friend; the two in tandem
Make and unmake dreams, like the nightingale's
    Sweet song conjuring a vision, then fading,
Or the hope-filled waves rising, breaking, rising.

So, my Love, with you I dream; I dream
Of love we've had and shared; I dream, too,
    Of love unspoken, unrealized,
To be fulfilled when Day comes, beyond night.

Sheep Bells

The sheep on the green field
Are sprinkled like salt crystals on a tablecloth.
Their bells tinkle in the darkening air
Like words you've whispered in my ear at night,
Like words you spoke by the sea
On the coast of Crete
When we were young.
Shafts of rough cloud reach toward me from the veiled sun,
Beams like fingers, like a hand,
Like a hand from once.
I hear words,
Yours.
The hand pulls back,
Dissolves.
The sheep are placid in the dusk.
Their bells tinkle,
One, then another,
Then all together:
Notes like starlight,
Counterpoint to the susurrus of waves
(Whispers in the night),
When we walked along the rocky coast
Beside the ancient sea.
I hear your words far off,

They tinkle like sheep bells.
They are starlight,
Bright speech.
And I hear the waves whispering,
Whispering in the night:
Love.
Your voice.

You

I

Pictures of you surround me.
A formal portrait before I knew you:
Glamour with a pearl necklace,
Light-filled eyes
Pure like pools,
Alert,
Reflecting sea, earth, grass,
Eyes expectant,
Open to love,
Open to God before you came to know Him,
Open like windows welcoming birds.
Your fine nose is rounded gently;
Your mouth is a peach-slice;
Your teeth, like small piano keys,
Rest between your smiling lips.

II

And here you are in Crete
Entering our hut by the sea,
Yellow dress showing off your cello-shape,
Blond hair water-falling down;
And here now at a stone basin washing clothes,
Nearby to our hut by the sea,
Sitting askew on the low wall,
Red dress,
Blond hair water-falling down.

III

Puy del Claux, Lot, France.
You are framed by heavy walls,
Pressed against thick stone,
The pale field opening out behind you.
You are fragility itself.
Yet what strength!
What womanhood!
The sun in your hair,
A wave of light!
Your smile is very joy putting out its sign:
"Laughter is what we do here: welcome!"

Drunk

I've been drunk twice.
The circumstances were quite different.
The first time, I was young.
I'd been to a party.
As in a dream, I was driving home late at night
In a Volkswagon Beetle.
Suddenly a huge red moon
Rose all at once in front of me.
It was like an enormous begonia.
Instinctively I slammed on the brakes
To avoid crashing into it.
At the same moment a Buick
Hurtled out of the night from my left
And crossed my bow.
Seconds later the begonia turned green.

My second experience was thirty-five years later.
An ordained minister with a DPhil from Oxford,
I was dining with my delightful wife
At a fine Parisian restaurant
Where the wine was offered for wholesale prices.
I had debts at the time, my salary was slim,
And friends had offered us this dinner for my birthday.

"The wine-list is excellent," our friends told us.
"Be sure to take advantage of the low prices."
We duly ordered two bottles of wine,
A red and a white.
Our conversation accelerated as we picked our way
Through the underbrush of the first course
(Shrimp and avocado in a creamy sauce),
As if we were heading excitedly toward base camp
For a Himalayan ascent.
We started up the mountain of the meat course with vigour,
Our voices growing louder as we climbed.
We told stories and laughed and quaffed,
Then told more stories and laughed and quaffed.
The nearer we got to the summit of the *boeuf bourguignon*,
The louder we jabbered.
But at the summit our conversation slowed.
I was a bit woozy.
"It's the altitude," I told myself.
The bottle of red was empty.
As we started the descent toward dessert,
We opened the white wine and giggled.
We stumbled down the rough terrain
Of the last chunks of *boeuf bourguignon*,
Our heads in our plates,
Hardly talking.
When we reached the valley floor,
Half the white wine was gone.
Our minds were muddy.
The *crème caramel* was like skating on ice—
It revived us briefly.

We tried very hard to think the air was bracing us.
We emptied our glasses for the last time,
Then fell silent.
The two empty bottles observed us quizzically
From the middle of the table.
We skipped coffee.
I managed to sign my credit card,
Then swayed towards the door;
My wife, more sure-footed than I,
Followed apprehensively.
Just outside the entrance,
I tripped on the front step.
Ordained minister and Oxford DPhil,
I found myself sprawled face down on the pavement.
"Damn step is too high," I mumbled.
"…too high."
"Are you hurt?" cried my wife.
"No, no, it's nothing, nothing at all."
She helped me to my feet as quickly as she could.
"Oh dear, I hope you're not hurt."
"No, no, it's nothing— really."
In the taxi home my wife hugged me.
We didn't talk.

We thanked our friends effusively the next day.
"The meal was great!" we exclaimed.
"And the wine was terrific—off the charts!"
They beamed.
A few weeks later we had them for dinner
And told them the whole story.

I was their pastor at the time,
I had to come clean.
"Someday you'll have to write a poem about it,"
They said, unable to hide their amusement.
"Poetry can be a purgative, you've told us that yourself."
We had a good laugh.

And so I've written the poem—
Twenty years later.

Giggle

You notice the roll above my belt,
The pen lying on it happily
Like a sun-bather on a ledge.
"Look!" you cry, pointing.
"A shelf for your pen!" And your giggle
Ripples like a band striking up
(I'd die for your giggle),
While your eyes set to dancing a jig.
"A very narrow shelf," I quip,
Laughing despite myself. "My belt
Is extra tight, that's the problem."
At which your giggle scales new heights
And your eyes swell and gleam brightly
Like blue-green ponds at midday.
Oh, we did laugh! Even my "shelf"
Set to bouncing (a bit), and the pen
Fell off on the floor. We stopped giggling
At last, and grew quiet. "Ah," you sighed,
"I do love to giggle!" "And I love your giggle,"
I replied. "Our years are piling up," you answered.
"But, praise God, we're still children!"

By the Beach

We were sitting on a bench staring at the agitated ocean.
Gulls with pink legs and yellow beaks were bunched on a rock
nearby.
Two flapped off suddenly, catching an updraft.
Then a white furry dog appeared with three girls in tow,
And all four ran down the wet sand barking and giggling.
"Oh," you exclaimed, "it's wonderful the way dogs love their
people!"
I remembered Moose, you remembered Smokey and Thumper.
The parents appeared with a picnic basket, and the family of six
Settled in the beach-grass just out of reach of the wave-foam
Rolling up the sand in intersecting arcs.
The wet sand was the colour of walnuts,
The sand higher up was the colour of peanuts.
"I was a towhead when I was young," you said.
"In the summer I used to ride the waves on a mat."
"I did too," I said. "I'd catch them way out,
Just when they were cresting and beginning to break."
The white dog and the girls were skipping and jumping
At the water's edge where spent waves left foam-frills
quivering.
The frills were like memories.
"We were blessed," you said. "We had a childhood.
So many children today don't have a childhood."

"Everything is in upheaval today," I said.
"Childhood is disappearing."
We stared at the ocean in silence.
A half mile from shore waves were breaking
At the edge of a shelf of flat rock.
Combers rolled in at all angles according to the lay of the rock,
Leaving scattered behind them on the trampled sea-face
Torn flags and scarves of churned surf.
"Violence is everywhere," I said.
"Those children don't know that yet," you said.
"They're the exception today," I said.
The sound of the surf was an unbroken roar
Like the pedal point of an organ;
The wave-crash and hiss of the foam up the beach were like chords.
The music we were hearing was a fugue without end.
"When I was a child, the sound of the waves used to lull me to sleep," I said.
"It still does me," you said. "There's a child in us that never dies."
"Unless it's murdered," I said.
"But God can raise it up," you said.
The white dog and three girls were romping in the rubbery algae
That stretched along the beach like trails of cooked spinach.
On the sea-breeze, in moments of wave-calm,
Along with the salt and the smell of the seaweed,
Their sharp barks and squeals of laughter reached our ears.
The parents were watching from their shelter in the beach grass.
"That's a family," I said.

"They love each other," you said.
We stared in silence at the tumultuous ocean
And listened to the roar of the fugue without end.
The waves and wind and the sea symphony,
And the cormorants diving,
And the white furry dog and the girls giggling,
And the parents carefully preparing the picnic,
Eased our hearts.
We were children again.
"It's a taste of eternal life," you said.
We laughed,
The girls laughed,
The waves tossed and tumbled,
Laughing.

Rainstorm

Night, a four-lane highway.
Rain is beating on the windscreen with angry fists.
The galley-slave wipers, under the whip-crack of thunder, row desperately.
Headlights move towards us in slow motion,
Probing the darkness like the antennae of snails.
Cars pulled over in the emergency lane hulk in our headlights
Like wrecks thrown on reefs.
We decide not to stop despite low visibility.
You are at the wheel, intense.
I encourage you, watchful.
You don't waver.
"You're doing a great job," I say.
"I'm trying," you say.
Just then a gust slams the car and rain sluices over the glass
Like a river flooding a street suddenly.
I feel your hands tighten on the wheel.
You don't waver.
The wipers take control again.
"You're doing a great job," I repeat.
"Thanks. That was quite a blast."
"Yup."
We pull up on a truck lumbering along.

Four red lights.
"Follow it," I say.
"Stay back from the spray, but track it.
Keep in its wake."
I can feel us breathing again.
"Now we can see the road, right?"
"Yes."
"Stay behind the truck."
"Don't worry."
The tail-lights guide us for miles.
At last the rain lets up.
We pick up speed and overtake the truck.
As we pass it, you flash our lights:
"Thanks!"
"We made it!" I cry as we move into the night.
"You did a great job, Love!"
"Thank God for the truck," you murmur.
"Yes—the four red lights."
"Yes."

Youth

I cannot match the genius of the Bard,
Who ranged his lines against the rule of time;
Yet saving you from age should not be hard,
If, to your youth, I could match my rhyme.
For youth is not time's toy to break, as though
Revolving nature had the final say;
Beauty's a gift God chooses to bestow
On those who live by grace and walk His Way.
So far from miring you in cumbrous age,
The train of years, unfreighting you, has shed
Your ballast, till now, lightly, you turn each page
Of time with a swift glance, and fly ahead.
In this you give the lie to death's decree,
And keep your youth into eternity.

Her Life Has Been a Flower

In our tunnel, there is light.
It is not my light, though it blesses me.
It is the light of the memory of flowers.

Daffodils gathered round her childhood:
Wild on the hills, intimate in planted gardens.

Her youth wore irises,
Flouncy dresses at galas;
Her comeliness lured bees;
Her mind roamed the world on words.

Then poppies burst,
Papering the fields orange.
These were embers from old stars
Left over from the beginning of creation:
Here God's love burned hotly.

And then came plethoras of roses,
Opening like cupped hands:
Angelic hierarchies petalled together in praise.
Their perfume joined the lavender in evening
To inundate the nostrils,
Like surf flushing into sea-caves:
Intoxication.

In age, at the turning, where the road entered the tunnel,
It was fallen leaves,
The tans and coffee-browns where once green reigned.
With wonder she stooped to pick them up
From city streets and gutters and weedy waysides,
Anywhere, everywhere,
Leaves that used to ride the waves of the wind,
Applaud enthusiastically mellifluous birds,
Whisper sweet nothings to the moon.

And now we walk together in our tunnel
Toward a greater Light.
She gathers wildflowers ceaselessly:
Daisies, bugloss, buttercups, yarrow, cowslips.
The smaller the bud, the more she marvels,
Marvels at the tints, the shapes, the curls, the whorls,
As she marvels to see a beetle with red and black stripes
Labouring to climb a grass-blade,
Or a fly batting a window pane helplessly—
Which immediately prompts her to open the window to save it.
"It's a critter, it does good work, God made it!"
How happy it makes her to save a fly!
Perhaps she knows what it feels.

Her life has been a flower,
From bud to swell to nectared bloom:
Countless bees and creatures of all sorts
Have tasted her pollen and rejoiced.
And they rejoice now and will go on rejoicing,
For she will give off her sweet aroma forever.

Silence

I must find images now,
The plain word for the plain thing
Won't do any more.
As age shrinks me,
And the dear one closest to me,
I must find a new equilibrium.
Where once words conjured dreams
Or elaborated the patterns of clouds
Or considered conceptual paradigms,
Now silence lies like the light of the setting sun
On still-warm fields,
Where creatures tired from the scramble of life
Prepare to bed down for the night.

We too must prepare to bed down for the night.
When words are reduced to infrequent visits,
It is like a home emptied of its children.
If you listen closely,
You can hear the laughter of the children who have left.
Inside the silence, the air is close;
It can be hard to draw breath.
Yet love is finding new expressions too,
So that the silence,

While being absence,
Is also presence.
The communion that always underlay
The words we shared
Has risen from the deep
And lies now on the surface, naked,
As when two souls inside two pairs of eyes
Undress and behold each other truly,
With wonder.
In this simplicity,
What words we speak are like islands
In an ocean of silence.
There is emptiness,
There is fullness.
Weakness erodes our mortal lives,
The artifacts of time;
But the hard stone of eternity,
Granitic,
Stands forth boldly
And will endure.

Contrails, Clouds, Sky

You loved to point out contrails
Running up and down the blue sky
Like lines of chalk.
"There are people up there in those planes!"
You'd exclaim in amazement.
Perhaps, as your mind began to leave you,
You wanted to be up there with those people.
You loved the shapes of clouds.
You'd talk about cumulus and cirrus
And point out bears and crocodiles and camels,
All fighting and eating each other.
But it was make-believe, so you just laughed,
You who were so inconsolable at displays of cruelty.
Perhaps the game lifted up your anxious heart.
You loved the sky at sunset,
When pinks and oranges wove oriental carpets
On the western horizon.
You always saw pink when I saw orange.
You'd watch contrails turn into clouds
As the planes sped north or east to far-away places.
Perhaps you longed to be up there with the passengers,
Flying to heaven.

Eyes of Love

When I behold you with the eyes of love,
I see God's radiance in your lovely face.
In your eyes shines pure light from high above
Our realm, where earth's cloistered pastures give place
To open range, everlasting, boundless.
Of that realm, in your eyes' depths, I see the gleam,
Like a spark echoing the fire in the furnace
Of a distant star, as in a vivid dream
One might experience the wild glory
Of divinity unleashed. That gleam tells
Of your great Maker, speaks the story
Of His profligate love drawn from the wells
Of His primordial Life. In your lovely face
God's love is mirrored, figuring His grace.

The Smile

At her mouth's edge a smile dawns.
Like sunlight through broken clouds gliding on a grassy hill,
It moves across her lips silently,
Even as her mind's motions
Recall a joke, a jest, a shared intimacy,
And pull up into light
A forgotten thread from our love.
Her lips part,
Sun floods the hill,
The smile breaks over her face like a wave—
She *laughs*.
Her eyes flash like pools on the hillside,
Her heart erupts—
And for a moment there is no time,
Time has gone over the hill,
It has vanished.
There is only *now*,
Eternity.
Joy

Bar-Code

My muse has lost her voice
(For now),
So I am mute.
How shall I speak?
Oh, I would be the window-ledge
Upon which frost sews doilies
Every night!
I would be the bluebell sky
Upon which clouds unroll prophetic scrolls
On winter afternoons!
My road displays a bar-code
Cast by shadows of the long-trunked trees
That line my route—
Who will read it?
I've been told my way is love—
I've been shown this by the Lord I serve.
But how shall I, poor aging soul,
Show love befitting her
To my sweet mate
(For love, to be true,
Must fit the object loved
And be not just the subject's wish)?
How shall I,

Who so fear loss,
Resist my fear of what must someday come?
"By loving," says my Lord.
"One loves today,
Not yesterday, not the day to come.
Love is in the things you see
And in your gestures,
Your gentle gestures.
The doily on the window-pane each day
Is love;
The sky's white scrolls
Are love;
The bar-code I, the Lord, have laid across your heart
Is love."
O Muse—*bless you*!

The Offering

There is no wind,
Not a puff.
Not a leaf on the scrub-oaks quivers.
No wrinkles trouble the puddles from the recent rain.
The trees stand still and stiff,
Wearing thick winter overcoats of ivy.
You are picking tiny purple flowers from the roadside,
I am studying the moss on the rough walls bordering the fields.
The moss wraps the rocks in soft green,
Tenderly,
Like a woman embracing her beloved.
Nature is quiet.
No birds swoop,
No wings flap.
No sound.
A few clouds float in the blue sea above our heads.
A fringe of oaks,
Like a child's scribbles,
Spans the hills swelling on the southern horizon.
Brambles weave a mesh of thorns around the lumpy fields.
Light fills the air.
The old broken oak near the spring is bent in prayer;
With all God's creatures, it hallows its Creator.

God is holding His breath,
His love fills the air.
He is listening.
We too are listening.
In the silence,
We hear Him.
You lift your head and offer Him joyfully
The tiny purple flowers;
I bow my head and offer Him joyfully
The green moss.
We offer our Creator what He has made.
With the hills, the trees, the rocks,
The thorny brambles, the lumpy earth,
We offer Him ourselves.

My Beloved Has Come Home
(after two and a half months in hospital)

The straggly hair of oak-trees tells me it is winter.
My beloved has come home.
We are playing the *adagio* of our Last Quartet—
Will there be an *allegro*?
Our Lord knows.
My beloved's feet hurt when she walks;
No shoes fit, she shuffles.
Her back aches when she sits.
She is tired.
But she doesn't give up,
She is brave.
She resumes her tasks.
Her brain is a worksite;
God Inc. (Incorporated) is her Contractor,
He is rebuilding her brain brick by brick,
Neuron by neuron.
The completion date is unclear.
His ways are not our ways.
My beloved sleeps a lot.
I join her. Long nights. *Adagio*.
And why not? It's enjoyable.
Ah, but when she wakes—those eyes!
Green of river-weed,

Brown of ploughed fields,
A wash of cornflower blue—
Jewels!
Here her soul laughs.
And now, glance lower:
Her breasts are aubergines,
Awaiting my mouth;
Her belly is a sward of flesh—joy!
And then the woods below,
Where my fingers walk at will;
And finally the lurking cave,
Where I poke and penetrate
In hot weather.
Ah!
My beloved's body is mine to love.
It is beauty,
Soul-haunted.
It exhibits spirit,
Like her eyes.
Oh, earnest atheist who might be reading these lines,
Do you really believe this creature is sheer Chance's bloom?
Be serious.
Leave your funhouse with its crazy mirrors,
Come outside into daylight,
Take off those silly dark glasses,
Take great gulps of air—
Look around!
And, I insist,
Should you see my lovely lady walking slowly
down a country lane,
Behold her and marvel!

Strange Dreams

It is the hour when men dream strange dreams
And stars watching at Earth's bedside
Wonder, meditatively, how long God
Will let our race languish in its nightmare.
For now, Night.
But, for now, I hear you beside me breathing.
Your body is next to mine.
In half-sleep our fingers lace.
I am not alone,
You are not alone.
I say to you: "Sweetheart."
In your half-sleep you murmur: "My lover is here."
Our fingers move like the fingers of one hand.
Night breathes too, like an enormous creature.
It creaks and rasps,
Whispers,
Hoots.
Its million eyes are diamonds mirroring Original Light,
As the eyes of my sweetheart lying beside me
Mirror her soul and her soul's Maker.
Do not try to imagine Night without stars,
Night that is just a *thing*, not a creature.
Those who dream strange dreams of Utter Dark will die.
When they start up in bed in the dead of night,

No one will be there to touch them,
No voice will be there in the darkness to whisper,
"I am here."

Has My Sun Set?

Oh, I've uttered fervent prayers, my God!
I've shot them like pellets, blown them like bubbles,
   Shaken them at you as I might shake a rod.
Day and night, Lord, I've poured out all my troubles.
 Anguished, I've cried to you for my beloved wife:
 God, breathe on the still-hot embers of her mind!
    Rekindle in those coals the fire of life!
 Bring mental light again where she's gone blind!
  You've heard me, Lord, I know that. Your ears
    Have not been closed, nor your heart. Yet,
    No answer comes. Despite my faith, fears
   Claw at me. I grow cold. Has my sun set?
   For my dear wife is like the sun to me.
    Have mercy, Lord—set Victoria free!

Winter Days

Moss blankets the stone walls like green snow.
It is eiderdown.
It rounds the rough rocks
The way a woman who loves a man
Rounds his angles and edges.
Windless winter days:
Not a twig quivers,
Even in the feathery tree-tips.
Blackbirds pepper the fields,
A few birds twitter in the hedges.
The roadside shrubs are a scraggly tangle,
The bramble leaves look like dried blood,
The berries in their thorn-beds are hard little nuggets.
The leaves on the scrub-oak have rusted;
Wizened trees wear ivy coats against the cold.
Gone are the oils of summer and autumn:
Winter is a pen and ink drawing.
In the mist-shrouded forest,
We are among the dead.
Gaunt trees stare, fleshless.
Phantoms.
Oh, these trees tossed their heads once,
They tossed their long hair once;

Now they look out from empty sockets.
A breath stirs the mist lightly,
The trees dissolve:
Time's bones picked clean.
Lichen the colour of sage is pasted in patches
On the fence-posts along the meadows.
A mustard-coloured lichen is slathered thickly
On the branches of briars and tree-trunks—
Walnut, hickory, oak—
Like pigment on a Rouault portrait.
Cries of long-ago summers echo here,
When we laughed together in the bright blue air.
Elsewhere colour has gone to leaf-mush
Or the gray of wave-tossed flotsam.
And now softly,
Softly,
Floating from the sky like memories,
Each flake a tear-drop,
Snow begins to settle on my broken heart.

Alone

The shadow of the leafless tree
On the wall of the white house
Is flat: a scrawl, weightless.
This is how my heart is
Without Victoria beside me:
I am the shadow of a leafless tree.
Nearby is a house boarded up,
The windows shuttered, blank.
This is how my heart is
Without Victoria beside me:
I am a shuttered pane of glass.

A single garden chair is tipped against a wall below me—
Just one chair, alone, tipped so the water won't collect on the seat.
I think of the twin chairs on our balcony,
Perched among the terra cotta tiles where a robin nests each May.
We used to sit there in the evening
And watch the sky become a painting
And then darken slowly into night and stars.
Shall we ever sit there again?

Along the roof-edge of a shed near the road,
Icicles hang like stilettos.
It is thawing.
Under plaques of ice still clinging to the moss,
Water creeps down the dark volcanic rocks by the road.
Billows floating in the blue air above me
Mirror the still-white hill-tops that cap the grassy slopes
Where the snow is draining off into the valley.
Will my slopes be green again someday?

Bare trees lining the hedgerows on the hills
Stand stiffly at attention like soldiers,
Their shadows floating at an angle on the snow below,
As if unmoored.
I am such a shadow, unmoored.
The hills are strewn with fishnets, string, wire.
Can you imagine living trees becoming wire?
High on a crest sits a scraggly ball of twine:
What is bleaker than a lonely oak in winter?

The Seed's Travail

The weeping willow in winter is yellow
Like the islands of lichen afloat on the seas
Of the cold calcareous walls of gray stone
That rim the brown fields lying fallow in sleep.
The seeds sunk in earth quietly slumber,
Nourishing life through the travail of death.
Thus lies my hope in the darkness of winter,
Awaiting new life in the great bloom of spring.
Shall this hope bloom in my earthly life *now*?
Shall my life's love be returned to me *here*?
Or must she die in the soil of this world
And her bloom be her bloom in the Kingdom of God?
I cry to my God to lift her from winter,
To give her new life for a few happy years.
But whatever awaits me, Lord: "Thy will be done.
Give me grace in my grief if her course here is run."

The Filly, the Wood Lark, the Woman

I

When I first saw my love,
She was like a filly fenced inside a ring
And taught to go round and round inside the ring.
I found her going round and round inside the ring,
Circling among her peers nervously,
An uneasy smile on her face,
And I knew instantly this was not her place,
Her heart was not here in the ring,
Her heart was in the high grasslands of the world
Where horses run wild and free
And gallop mile after mile with the fierce winds.
I drew her to my side
I drew her out of the ring
Our Creator joined our hearts in a lasting love
He joined our bodies
And we two ran together
On the high grasslands of the world.

II

Oh, we were not free entirely,
We were not free at first to offer ourselves entirely
To each other and to God.
Wounds and fears and inhibitions
Weren't cleared away instantly
When we left the ring.
Her scrupulosity needed tempering,
My intemperance needed taming.
Pride stalked us,
But *differently*.
My rages in our early years
And my negligence towards her later—
At a period when my hunger for knowledge obsessed me—
Stoked rejection in her
And made her vulnerable to self-deception.
For a time I left my love in a dry place,
I failed to water her heart,
I failed to nourish her body and soul.
Lacking protection, she lay exposed to passing gusts.
A sense of superiority in matters spiritual
And a passionate desire to right flaws
Opened her to illusion.
The weakness in each of us made the other vulnerable.
Oh, we were trapeze artists striving to perform,
Straining to fulfill our natures,
But God was bringing into light things hidden,

Revising our souls,
Reducing self-bondage.
Yes, the divine net caught us when we fell,
The divine hand drew good from our tumbles—
But we came away limping.

III

Nor did other sorrow spare us,
For children were not given us.
No little voices cried "Mummy!", "Daddy!",
No little persons jumped up and down and hugged us.
Oh, we did not want for friends in life,
We had a dozen godchildren,
But we never had a baby to cuddle,
We never had a child to put to bed.

IV

Ah, but our love—
Our *love*!
Under our turbulent surface,
Under the disorder,
Our love did not weaken.
From the first it had been a revelation,
And it sustained us.
Each, deep down, still dreamed the other,
Saw the other orbed in light as in a vision.

We never doubted that we were gifts, each to the other.
In offering ourselves, we found ourselves.
Through pain our love was earthed,
We discovered who we really were,
The ups and downs, the ins and outs—
We came to know each other honestly,
We came to serve each other humbly.
We learned to encourage,
We learned to forgive.
So our dream was made concrete,
It was purged by truth;
Our two-dimensional passion
Became a three-dimensional home.

V

And as God refined us,
As he deepened and matured us,
How we did exult in the fresh air we were breathing!
How we did laugh!
Intoxicated, we galloped joyfully,
The fierce wind in our faces.
Yes, sometimes we still lost our way,
Sometimes we disappointed each other,
Sometimes we tripped and fell headlong,
But we picked ourselves up and kept galloping,
Breathing hard,
Full of hope,
Full of life.
God held us tight.

VI

My filly was a thoroughbred.
Class!
She had *style*.
Her speech was like spring water welling up effortlessly;
Tropes abounded in it like coloured fish.
Her wit was like a fountain in an Italian piazza.
She wore mini-skirts and pumpkin-coloured scarves
(Among other things)
And wound her flaxen hair in a French twist.
Her eyes were beryls,
Created in deep earth and reflecting sky.
I would look in them and see myself being loved.
All of her invited me:
Her lips were sections of blood orange,
She painted them pink-red.
High brow, high cheekbones,
A fine neck,
Her shoulders and upper chest
Spreading outward, downward,
Like a talus.
Her upper arms were tubes of flesh,
Soft and firm;
Her forearms and wrists were slender shafts.
Her breasts were twin coconuts
Hung below the strands of her falling hair
(Her nipples drew my mouth like magnets);
Her belly was a pillow to lay my face on,
Her buttocks invited my hands.

She had the long legs of a thoroughbred filly,
Perfectly tapered,
And at their place of joining below her navel
Grew a forest delightful to enter.

VII

My love was a Wood Lark
Who called to me in the night;
Her clear voice came from a great distance,
As from the end of the world.
She called me to myself,
She made me sing;
And in my song
She discovered herself.
Hearing our calls in the night of the world,
Singing our songs,
We found ourselves each in the other.
Oh, wildly our hearts began to beat!
Arm in arm we jigged and waltzed!
Together we danced into the traffic of life,
Leaving loneliness behind us by the roadside.

VIII

And now: consider *woman*,
Consider this ineffable marvel of beauty,
This marvel like mist in a hidden valley
Hovering over a river at daybreak.

I quiver to see her:
The roundness,
The roll,
The swells, hollows,
Smoothness,
Softness,
Purity of form beyond description,
Beyond our words as far as stars lie beyond our earth.
O *woman*!
You are clematis in April blooming in doorways,
Lavender scenting evening air,
Flouncy iris flaunting your hips,
Tulips opening your mouths,
Eve before the Fall,
Innocent,
Naked,
Luscious.
You are fine wine to the palate,
Jasmine to the nostrils;
Your swaying movement enthralls—
Enchantress!
O *female*—I, *male*, hunger to know you,
To devour your flesh,
To devour the fruit of your flesh:
I hunger for the one like me and unlike me:
Bone of my bone,
Flesh of my flesh,
Soul-mate, companion, lover—
Woman.

IX

And now, consider *this* woman,
This *particular* woman,
This female who is *for me*,
My woman.
Thus the marvel of *love*,
When the male eye narrows its focus onto *one* woman
And intensifies the sun's light till fire breaks out.
I hunger for *this* woman,
I hunger to know her,
To lose myself inside her,
To enter her and become one with her
In an ecstasy of orgasm
Where both are utterly beyond ourselves
And utterly ourselves,
The completion of love in an overwhelming eruption
That is at once an unspeakable transcendence of earthliness
And the plenitude of earth's potency,
The image and fulfilment of earth's vocation
To be matter inspirited,
Sacrament of God's Kingdom,
Host of Christ's reign with his Bride—
You and I two yet one,
Plurality and unity,
The generic and the particular,
Man/woman,
This man/*this* woman,
Integrated perfectly in consuming love.
O *marvel*!
O *glory*!

X

This incandescent creation of God
Is the foretaste and image of heaven
That you and I have glimpsed and touched and tasted,
Dear Filly of mine, dear Wood Lark.
This is no mere ideal—
It is grace,
Grace fulfilling nature,
Perfecting God's gift.
As we age now, my darling,
My jaunty darling,
I am grateful to God who gave me *you*,
Who gave me *you* to love,
You whom I loved from the moment I saw you;
I am grateful to you who loved me from the beginning,
Who called me out of my night,
Who gave yourself to me;
I am grateful that I have known love and given love
In these years here on earth;
I am grateful that you and I shall love forever
In God's imperishable Life.

We Shall All Be Changed

How can it be these lambent eyes should fade
One day? As much to think the sky-charged sea
Should no more wear the fleecy clouds inlaid
    Upon its depths, or the planet cease to be!
How could these brows above her eyes, these roofs
    Sheltering doves, droop and fall beneath
The weight of furrowed age, the stamping hooves
    Of time, and moulder broken in the earth?
This smile, warm hammock stretched beneath her cheeks,
    In which her teeth like matching cushions lie,
Must close one dreadful day: but when He speaks
Who loves her, she'll smile anew, no more to die.
    For death is but a door to richer life
For those who long for God, like my dear wife.

www.ingramcontent.com/pod-product-compliance
Lightning Source LLC
Chambersburg PA
CBHW071743090426
42738CB00011B/2551